My grandpa is a fix-it man.
He can fix anything!

I love to watch Grandpa work
in his shop.

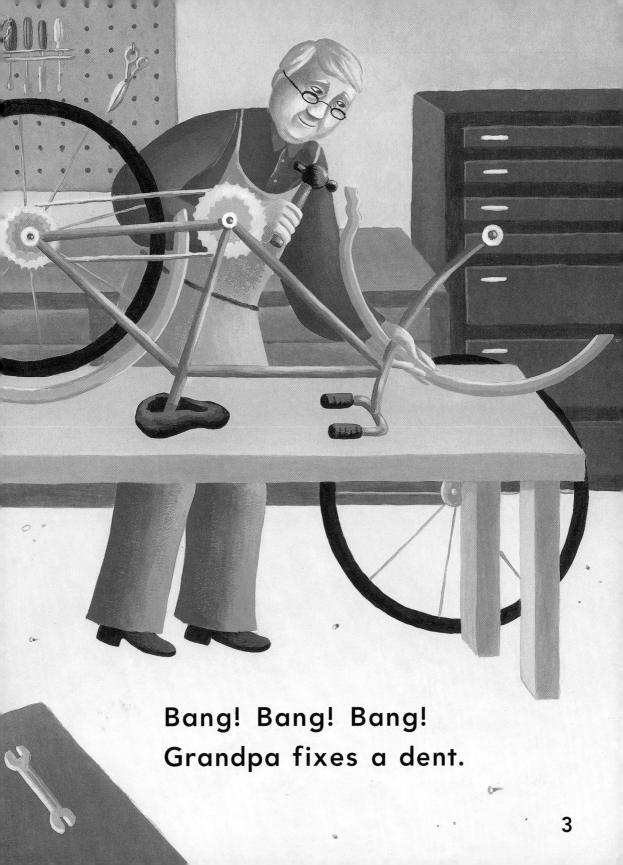

Bang! Bang! Bang!
Grandpa fixes a dent.

Buzz! Buzz! Buzz!
Grandpa saws a new leg
for a desk.

One day, I ask Grandpa
if I can help. He gives me
a long, flat piece of wood.
"Hold this," Grandpa says.

I hold the wood. Grandpa fits
it in a slot.

Soon we have a shelf!

"A fix-it girl needs a place for her things," says Grandpa.